THIS PLANT JOURNAL

Belongs To:

_____

How to use this Plant Journal

Use this planner to keep track of your pride and joy - all your special house plants! You can record and log details about each plant in your collection: what species, name, when you got it, what sort of sunlight and moisture it prefers, even if it's pet-friendly or not.

You'll also find included a handy schedule section not only for what plants you need to water and when, but also schedule and keep track of fertilization efforts. Even keep a plant wishlist of all those you can't wait to add to the plant family!

Watering Schedule

Month: _____

Plant Name	M	T	W	Th	F	S	Su

Notes

_____
_____
_____
_____
_____
_____

Watering Schedule

Month: _____

Plant Name	M	T	W	Th	F	S	Su

Notes

Watering Schedule

Month: _____

Plant Name	M	T	W	Th	F	S	Su

Notes

_____

_____

_____

_____

_____

_____

Watering Schedule

Month: _____

Plant Name	M	T	W	Th	F	S	Su

Notes

_____

_____

_____

_____

_____

Watering Schedule

Month: _____

Plant Name	M	T	W	Th	F	S	Su

Notes

_____

_____

_____

_____

_____

_____

Watering Schedule

Month: _____

Plant Name	M	T	W	Th	F	S	Su

Notes

_____

_____

_____

_____

_____

Watering Schedule

Month: _____

Plant Name	M	T	W	Th	F	S	Su

Notes

_____
_____
_____
_____
_____

Watering Schedule

Month: _____

Plant Name	M	T	W	Th	F	S	Su

Notes

_____

_____

_____

_____

_____

Watering Schedule

Month: _____

Plant Name	M	T	W	Th	F	S	Su

Notes

Watering Schedule

Month: _____

Plant Name	M	T	W	Th	F	S	Su

Notes

_____

_____

_____

_____

_____

_____

Watering Schedule

Month: _____

Plant Name	M	T	W	Th	F	S	Su

Notes

Watering Schedule

Month: _____

Plant Name	M	T	W	Th	F	S	Su

Notes

Let's go on an
ADVENTURE!
And by that I
mean let's go to
the **plant** store.

Fertilizing Schedule

Month: _____

Plant Name	M	T	W	Th	F	S	Su

Notes

Fertilizing Schedule

Month: _____

Plant Name	M	T	W	Th	F	S	Su

Notes

_____

_____

_____

_____

_____

Fertilizing Schedule

Month: _____

Plant Name	M	T	W	Th	F	S	Su

Notes

_____

_____

_____

_____

Fertilizing Schedule

Month: _____

Plant Name	M	T	W	Th	F	S	Su

Notes

Fertilizing Schedule

Month: _____

Plant Name	M	T	W	Th	F	S	Su

Notes

_____

_____

_____

_____

_____

Fertilizing Schedule

Month: _____

Plant Name	M	T	W	Th	F	S	Su

Notes

Fertilizing Schedule

Month: _____

Plant Name	M	T	W	Th	F	S	Su

Notes

Fertilizing Schedule

Month: _____

Plant Name	M	T	W	Th	F	S	Su

Notes

_____

_____

_____

_____

Fertilizing Schedule

Month: _____

Plant Name	M	T	W	Th	F	S	Su

Notes

_____

_____

_____

_____

_____

Fertilizing Schedule

Month: _____

Plant Name	M	T	W	Th	F	S	Su

Notes

_____

_____

_____

_____

_____

Fertilizing Schedule

Month: _____

Plant Name	M	T	W	Th	F	S	Su

Notes

_____
_____
_____
_____
_____

Fertilizing Schedule

Month: _____

Plant Name	M	T	W	Th	F	S	Su

Notes

_____

_____

_____

_____

_____

My favorite plant is:

_____

_____

Because:

_____

_____

_____

_____

_____

_____

Your Plant's Name: Gold Dust Croton

Scientific Name: Codiaeum

Date Acquired: 6/25/20   Plant #: _____

[X] Used Fertilizer?

[ ] Pet Friendly? NO

[ ] Indoor   [X] Outdoor

Water

Sunlight
NO direct
Sunlight during
midday.

- Subtropical, native to S. Asia,
- Also called "Sun spot croton"
- Medium pace grower, reaches heights between 4'-10' tall.
- 60°-85°F move inside when temp is below 50°
- Keep soil moist, but no standing water.
- Fertilize Weekly during growing periods.
- Likes slightly acidic soil.
- Repot in spring if needed.
- Likes to be trimmed if growth has become slow.
- Propagation? yes, cut 5-6 inches from new (4-6 weeks) growth and place in soil. Cover with bag to retain water.

Notes
Large Gold Dust bought at Walmart for $12! Fertilized the day I got it. I fertilized and watered with fish emulsions. this one will stay outdoors during the summer. Be sure to watch temparature drops at night to pull inside.

Your Plant's Name: Golden Pothos

Scientific Name: _____

Date Acquired: 05/03/20   *Plant #:* _____

☒ Used Fertilizer?

☐ Pet Friendly? NO

☒ Indoor   ☐ Outdoor

Water 💧 💧💧 💧💧

Sunlight ☀ ☀ ☀

Notes

Your Plant's Name: Neon Pathos

Scientific Name: _____

Date Acquired: 05/03/20   Plant #: _____

☒ Used Fertilizer?

☐ Pet Friendly? NO

☒ Indoor   ☐ Outdoor

Water 💧 💧💧 💧💧💧

Sunlight ☀ ☀ ☀

Notes

Your Plant's Name: Marble Queen

Scientific Name: Epipremnum Aureum

Date Acquired: 05/03/20   Plant #: _____

- [ ] Used Fertilizer?

- [ ] Pet Friendly? NO

- [X] Indoor   [ ] Outdoor

Water

Sunlight

- Dry soil. Let dry out 50% during grow season and completely during winter.
- 65°- 85°F.
- Like to be rootbound.
- Prune to help growth, propagate the clippings.
- #2 toxicity level, keep away from pets and children.
- Fertilize every other month.

Notes

As of 06/25 I am battling gnats. Using neem oil to try to reduce the issue. Moved plant to the bathroom to quarantine. Plant is still producing new growth.

Your Plant's Name: <u>Swiss Cheese Plant</u>

Scientific Name: <u>Monstera adansonii</u>

Date Acquired: <u>05/03/20</u>   *Plant #:* _____

[X] **Used Fertilizer?**

[ ] **Pet Friendly?** NO

[ ] **Indoor**   [ ] **Outdoor**

Water 💧 (💧💧) 💧💧

Sunlight ☀ (☀) ☀
° likes humidity

- Tropical, native to South and Central America.
- Loves to climb.
- Moderately toxic to pets.

Notes

_____
_____
_____
_____
_____
_____
_____

Your Plant's Name: _____

Scientific Name: _____

Date Acquired: _____ *Plant #:* _____

☐ Used Fertilizer?

☐ Pet Friendly?

☐ Indoor ☐ Outdoor

Water 💧 💧💧 💧💧💧

Sunlight ☀ ☀ ☀

Notes

_____
_____
_____
_____
_____
_____
_____

Your Plant's Name: _____

Scientific Name: _____

Date Acquired: _____   Plant #: _____

☐ Used Fertilizer?

☐ Pet Friendly?

☐ Indoor   ☐ Outdoor

Water 💧 💧💧 💧💧

Sunlight ☀ ☀ ☀

Notes

Your Plant's Name: _____

Scientific Name: _____

Date Acquired: _____ *Plant #:* _____

☐ Used Fertilizer?

☐ Pet Friendly?

☐ Indoor   ☐ Outdoor

Water 💧 💧💧 💧💧

Sunlight ☀ ☀ ☀

Notes

Your Plant's Name: _____

Scientific Name: _____

Date Acquired: _____ *Plant #:* _____

☐ Used Fertilizer?

☐ Pet Friendly?

☐ Indoor   ☐ Outdoor

Water 💧 💧💧 💧💧

Sunlight ☀ ☀ ☀

Notes

_____
_____
_____
_____
_____
_____
_____
_____

Your Plant's Name: _____

Scientific Name: _____

Date Acquired: _____ *Plant #:* _____

☐ Used Fertilizer?

☐ Pet Friendly?

☐ Indoor ☐ Outdoor

Water 💧 💧💧 💧💧💧

Sunlight ☀ ☀ ☀

Notes

_____
_____
_____
_____
_____
_____
_____
_____

Your Plant's Name: _____

Scientific Name: _____

Date Acquired: _____ Plant #: _____

☐ Used Fertilizer?   Water   💧 💧💧 💧💧

☐ Pet Friendly?   Sunlight   ☀ ☀ ☀

☐ Indoor   ☐ Outdoor

Notes
_____
_____
_____
_____
_____
_____
_____
_____

Your Plant's Name: _____

Scientific Name: _____

Date Acquired: _____ *Plant #:* _____

☐ **Used Fertilizer?**

☐ **Pet Friendly?**

☐ **Indoor**   ☐ Outdoor

Water   💧   💧💧   💧💧💧

Sunlight   ☀   ☀   ☀

Notes

Your Plant's Name: _____

Scientific Name: _____

Date Acquired: _____ *Plant #:* _____

- [ ] Used Fertilizer?
- [ ] Pet Friendly?
- [ ] Indoor [ ] Outdoor

Water 💧 💧💧 💧💧

Sunlight ☀ ☀ ☀

Notes

Your Plant's Name: _____

Scientific Name: _____

Date Acquired: _____   *Plant #:* _____

☐ Used Fertilizer?

☐ Pet Friendly?

☐ Indoor   ☐ Outdoor

Water 💧 💧💧 💧💧💧

Sunlight ✴ ✴ ✴

Notes

_____
_____
_____
_____
_____
_____
_____
_____

Your Plant's Name: _____

Scientific Name: _____

Date Acquired: _____ *Plant #:* _____

☐ Used Fertilizer?

☐ Pet Friendly?

☐ Indoor   ☐ Outdoor

Water 💧 💧💧 💧💧

Sunlight ☀ ☀ ☀

Notes

Your Plant's Name: _____

Scientific Name: _____

Date Acquired: _____ *Plant #:* _____

☐ Used Fertilizer?

☐ Pet Friendly?

☐ Indoor ☐ Outdoor

Water 💧 💧💧 💧💧

Sunlight ☀ ☀ ☀

Notes

Your Plant's Name: _____

Scientific Name: _____

Date Acquired: _____ Plant #: _____

- [ ] Used Fertilizer?
- [ ] Pet Friendly?
- [ ] Indoor [ ] Outdoor

Water 💧 💧💧 💧💧

Sunlight ☀ ☀ ☀

Notes

_____
_____
_____
_____
_____
_____
_____

Your Plant's Name: _____

Scientific Name: _____

Date Acquired: _____ *Plant #:* _____

☐ Used Fertilizer?

☐ Pet Friendly?

☐ Indoor   ☐ Outdoor

Water 💧 💧💧 💧💧

Sunlight ☀ ☀ ☀

Notes
_____
_____
_____
_____
_____
_____
_____
_____

Your Plant's Name: _____

Scientific Name: _____

Date Acquired: _____ Plant #: _____

- [ ] Used Fertilizer?

- [ ] Pet Friendly?

- [ ] Indoor   - [ ] Outdoor

Water

Sunlight

Notes

_____
_____
_____
_____
_____
_____
_____
_____

Your Plant's Name: _____

Scientific Name: _____

Date Acquired: _____   *Plant #:* _____

☐ Used Fertilizer?

☐ Pet Friendly?

☐ Indoor   ☐ Outdoor

Water 🌢 🌢🌢 🌢🌢🌢

Sunlight ☀ ☀ ☀

Notes

Your Plant's Name: _____

Scientific Name: _____

Date Acquired: _____   *Plant #:* _____

☐ Used Fertilizer?   Water   💧 💧💧 💧💧💧

☐ Pet Friendly?   Sunlight ☀ ☀ ☀

☐ Indoor   ☐ Outdoor

Notes

_____
_____
_____
_____
_____
_____
_____
_____

Your Plant's Name: _____

Scientific Name: _____

Date Acquired: _____ *Plant #:* _____

☐ Used Fertilizer?

☐ Pet Friendly?

☐ Indoor ☐ Outdoor

Water 💧 💧💧 💧💧💧

Sunlight ☀ ☀ ☀

Notes

_____
_____
_____
_____
_____
_____
_____
_____

Your Plant's Name: _____

Scientific Name: _____

Date Acquired: _____ *Plant #:* _____

☐ Used Fertilizer?

☐ Pet Friendly?

☐ Indoor   ☐ Outdoor

Water 💧 💧💧 💧💧💧

Sunlight ☀ ☀ ☀

Notes

Your Plant's Name: _____

Scientific Name: _____

Date Acquired: _____ *Plant #:* _____

☐ Used Fertilizer?

☐ Pet Friendly?

☐ Indoor ☐ Outdoor

Water 💧 💧💧 💧💧

Sunlight ☀ ☀ ☀

Notes

Your Plant's Name: _____

Scientific Name: _____

Date Acquired: _____   _Plant #:_ _____

☐ **Used Fertilizer?**

☐ **Pet Friendly?**

☐ **Indoor**   ☐ **Outdoor**

Water   💧   💧💧   💧💧

Sunlight   ☀   ☀   ☀

Notes

Your Plant's Name: _____

Scientific Name: _____

Date Acquired: _____   *Plant #:* _____

☐ Used Fertilizer?

☐ Pet Friendly?

☐ Indoor   ☐ Outdoor

Water   💧 💧💧 💧💧

Sunlight   ☀ ☀ ☀

Notes

_____

_____

_____

_____

_____

_____

_____

Your Plant's Name: _____

Scientific Name: _____

Date Acquired: _____ Plant #: _____

☐ Used Fertilizer?

☐ Pet Friendly?

☐ Indoor ☐ Outdoor

Water 💧 💧💧 💧💧

Sunlight ☀ ☀ ☀

Notes

Your Plant's Name: _____

Scientific Name: _____

Date Acquired: _____ Plant #: _____

☐ Used Fertilizer?

☐ Pet Friendly?

☐ Indoor   ☐ Outdoor

Water 💧 💧💧 💧💧

Sunlight ☀ ☀ ☀

Notes
_____
_____
_____
_____
_____
_____
_____

Your Plant's Name: _____

Scientific Name: _____

Date Acquired: _____   *Plant #:* _____

☐ Used Fertilizer?   Water   💧   💧💧   💧💧

☐ Pet Friendly?   Sunlight ☀   ☀   ☀

☐ Indoor   ☐ Outdoor

Notes

Your Plant's Name: _____

Scientific Name: _____

Date Acquired: _____ *Plant #:* _____

☐ Used Fertilizer?

☐ Pet Friendly?

☐ Indoor   ☐ Outdoor

Water 💧 💧💧 💧💧

Sunlight ☀ ☀ ☀

Notes

Your Plant's Name: _____

Scientific Name: _____

Date Acquired: _____ *Plant #:* _____

☐ Used Fertilizer?

☐ Pet Friendly?

☐ Indoor ☐ Outdoor

Water 💧 💧💧 💧💧

Sunlight ☀ ☀ ☀

Notes

Your Plant's Name: _____

Scientific Name: _____

Date Acquired: _____ *Plant #:* _____

☐ Used Fertilizer? Water 💧 💧💧 💧💧💧

☐ Pet Friendly? Sunlight ☀ ☀ ☀

☐ Indoor ☐ Outdoor

Notes

Your Plant's Name: _____

Scientific Name: _____

Date Acquired: _____ Plant #: _____

☐ Used Fertilizer?   Water   💧 💧💧 💧💧

☐ Pet Friendly?   Sunlight   ☀ ☀ ☀

☐ Indoor   ☐ Outdoor

Notes
_____
_____
_____
_____
_____
_____
_____

Your Plant's Name: _____

Scientific Name: _____

Date Acquired: _____ *Plant #:* _____

☐ Used Fertilizer?

☐ Pet Friendly?

☐ Indoor   ☐ Outdoor

Water 💧 💧💧 💧💧

Sunlight ☀ ☀ ☀

Notes

Your Plant's Name: _____

Scientific Name: _____

Date Acquired: _____ *Plant #:* _____

☐ Used Fertilizer?

☐ Pet Friendly?

☐ Indoor ☐ Outdoor

Water 💧 💧💧 💧💧

Sunlight ☀ ☀ ☀

Notes

Your Plant's Name: _____

Scientific Name: _____

Date Acquired: _____ *Plant #:* _____

☐ **Used Fertilizer?**

☐ **Pet Friendly?**

☐ Indoor   ☐ Outdoor

Water   💧 💧💧 💧💧

Sunlight   ☀ ☀ ☀

Notes

Your Plant's Name: _____

Scientific Name: _____

Date Acquired: _____ Plant #: _____

☐ Used Fertilizer?   Water   💧 💧💧 💧💧

☐ Pet Friendly?   Sunlight   ☀ ☀ ☀

☐ Indoor   ☐ Outdoor

Notes

Your Plant's Name: _____

Scientific Name: _____

Date Acquired: _____ _Plant #:_ _____

☐ **Used Fertilizer?**

☐ **Pet Friendly?**

☐ **Indoor** ☐ **Outdoor**

Water 💧 💧💧 💧💧💧

Sunlight ☀ ☀ ☀

Notes

Your Plant's Name: _____

Scientific Name: _____

Date Acquired: _____   *Plant #:* _____

☐ Used Fertilizer?

☐ Pet Friendly?

☐ Indoor   ☐ Outdoor

Water   💧   💧💧   💧💧

Sunlight   ✺   ✹   ✷

Notes

Your Plant's Name: _____

Scientific Name: _____

Date Acquired: _____ _Plant #:_ _____

☐ **Used Fertilizer?**   **Water**   🌢   🌢🌢   🌢🌢

☐ **Pet Friendly?**   **Sunlight**   ✷   ✷   ✷

☐ **Indoor**   ☐ **Outdoor**

Notes

_____
_____
_____
_____
_____
_____
_____
_____

Your Plant's Name: _____

Scientific Name: _____

Date Acquired: _____ Plant #: _____

☐ Used Fertilizer?

☐ Pet Friendly?

☐ Indoor ☐ Outdoor

Water 💧 💧💧 💧💧

Sunlight ☀ ☀ ☀

Notes

_____
_____
_____
_____
_____
_____
_____
_____

Your Plant's Name: _____

Scientific Name: _____

Date Acquired: _____ *Plant #:* _____

☐ Used Fertilizer?   Water 💧 💧💧 💧💧💧

☐ Pet Friendly?   Sunlight ✴ ✴ ✴

☐ Indoor   ☐ Outdoor

Notes

_____
_____
_____
_____
_____
_____
_____
_____

Your Plant's Name: _____

Scientific Name: _____

Date Acquired: _____   *Plant #:* _____

☐ Used Fertilizer?   Water   💧   💧💧   💧💧

☐ Pet Friendly?   Sunlight ☀   ☀   ☀

☐ Indoor   ☐ Outdoor

Notes

Your Plant's Name: _____

Scientific Name: _____

Date Acquired: _____ *Plant #:* _____

☐ Used Fertilizer? Water 💧 💧💧 💧💧

☐ Pet Friendly? Sunlight ✳ ✳ ✳

☐ Indoor ☐ Outdoor

Notes

Your Plant's Name: _____

Scientific Name: _____

Date Acquired: _____ *Plant #:* _____

☐ Used Fertilizer?

☐ Pet Friendly?

☐ Indoor ☐ Outdoor

Water 🌢 🌢🌢 🌢🌢

Sunlight ☀ ☀ ☀

Notes

_____
_____
_____
_____
_____
_____
_____

Your Plant's Name: _____

Scientific Name: _____

Date Acquired: _____ *Plant #:* _____

☐ Used Fertilizer?

☐ Pet Friendly?

☐ Indoor ☐ Outdoor

Water 💧 💧💧 💧💧

Sunlight ☀ ☀ ☀

Notes

_____
_____
_____
_____
_____
_____
_____
_____

Your Plant's Name: _____

Scientific Name: _____

Date Acquired: _____ Plant #: _____

☐ Used Fertilizer?

☐ Pet Friendly?

☐ Indoor   ☐ Outdoor

Water 💧 💧💧 💧💧

Sunlight ☀ ☀ ☀

Notes

_____
_____
_____
_____
_____
_____
_____
_____

Your Plant's Name: _____

Scientific Name: _____

Date Acquired: _____   *Plant #:* _____

☐ Used Fertilizer?   Water   💧 💧💧 💧💧💧

☐ Pet Friendly?   Sunlight ✴ ✴ ✴

☐ Indoor   ☐ Outdoor

Notes

_____
_____
_____
_____
_____
_____
_____

Your Plant's Name: _____

Scientific Name: _____

Date Acquired: _____ *Plant #:* _____

☐ Used Fertilizer?

☐ Pet Friendly?

☐ Indoor ☐ Outdoor

Water 💧 💧💧 💧💧

Sunlight ☀ ☀ ☀

Notes

_____
_____
_____
_____
_____
_____
_____
_____

Your Plant's Name: _____

Scientific Name: _____

Date Acquired: _____   *Plant #:* _____

☐ **Used Fertilizer?**

☐ **Pet Friendly?**

☐ **Indoor**   ☐ **Outdoor**

Water 💧 💧💧 💧💧💧

Sunlight ☀ ☀ ☀

Notes

Your Plant's Name: _____

Scientific Name: _____

Date Acquired: _____ *Plant #:* _____

☐ Used Fertilizer?

☐ Pet Friendly?

☐ Indoor   ☐ Outdoor

Water 💧 💧💧 💧💧

Sunlight ☀ ☀ ☀

Notes

Your Plant's Name: _____

Scientific Name: _____

Date Acquired: _____ *Plant #:* _____

☐ Used Fertilizer?   Water   💧 💧💧 💧💧

☐ Pet Friendly?   Sunlight   ✴ ✴ ✴

☐ Indoor   ☐ Outdoor

Notes

Your Plant's Name: _____

Scientific Name: _____

Date Acquired: _____ Plant #: _____

Used Fertilizer?

Pet Friendly?

Indoor ☐ Outdoor ☐

Water ● ●● ●●

Sunlight

Notes

Your Plant's Name: _____

Scientific Name: _____

Date Acquired: _____   _Plant #:_ _____

☐ **Used Fertilizer?**   Water   💧 💧💧 💧💧💧

☐ **Pet Friendly?**   Sunlight ✷ ✷ ✷

☐ Indoor   ☐ Outdoor

Notes

_____
_____
_____
_____
_____
_____
_____
_____

Your Plant's Name: _____

Scientific Name: _____

Date Acquired: _____   *Plant #:* _____

☐ Used Fertilizer?

☐ Pet Friendly?

☐ Indoor   ☐ Outdoor

Water 💧 💧💧 💧💧

Sunlight ☀ ☀ ☀

Notes

Your Plant's Name: _____

Scientific Name: _____

Date Acquired: _____ *Plant #:* _____

☐ Used Fertilizer?   Water 💧 💧💧 💧💧

☐ Pet Friendly?   Sunlight ✴ ✴ ✴

☐ Indoor   ☐ Outdoor

Notes

Your Plant's Name: _____

Scientific Name: _____

Date Acquired: _____   *Plant #:* _____

☐ Used Fertilizer?   Water   💧 💧💧 💧💧

☐ Pet Friendly?   Sunlight ✷ ✷ ✷

☐ Indoor   ☐ Outdoor

Notes

Your Plant's Name: _____

Scientific Name: _____

Date Acquired: _____   Plant #: _____

☐ Used Fertilizer?

☐ Pet Friendly?

☐ Indoor   ☐ Outdoor

Water 💧 💧💧 💧💧💧

Sunlight ☀ ☀ ☀

Notes

Your Plant's Name: _____

Scientific Name: _____

Date Acquired: _____ *Plant #:* _____

☐ Used Fertilizer?

☐ Pet Friendly?

☐ Indoor ☐ Outdoor

Water 💧 💧💧 💧💧

Sunlight ☀ ☀ ☀

Notes

Your Plant's Name: _____

Scientific Name: _____

Date Acquired: _____ *Plant #:* _____

☐ Used Fertilizer?

☐ Pet Friendly?

☐ Indoor ☐ Outdoor

Water 💧 💧💧 💧💧

Sunlight ☀ ☀ ☀

Notes

_____
_____
_____
_____
_____
_____
_____
_____

Your Plant's Name: _____

Scientific Name: _____

Date Acquired: _____   *Plant #:* _____

☐ Used Fertilizer?

☐ Pet Friendly?

☐ Indoor   ☐ Outdoor

Water   💧   💧💧   💧💧

Sunlight   ☀   ☀   ☀

Notes

Your Plant's Name: _____

Scientific Name: _____

Date Acquired: _____   *Plant #:* _____

☐ Used Fertilizer?   Water   💧 💧💧 💧💧💧

☐ Pet Friendly?   Sunlight   ☀ ☀ ☀

☐ Indoor   ☐ Outdoor

Notes

_____
_____
_____
_____
_____
_____
_____
_____

Your Plant's Name: _____

Scientific Name: _____

Date Acquired: _____   *Plant #:* _____

☐ Used Fertilizer?   Water   💧   💧💧   💧💧

☐ Pet Friendly?   Sunlight   ☀   ☀   ☀

☐ Indoor   ☐ Outdoor

Notes

Your Plant's Name: _____

Scientific Name: _____

Date Acquired: _____   *Plant #:* _____

☐ **Used Fertilizer?**   Water   💧 💧💧 💧💧

☐ **Pet Friendly?**   Sunlight   ✳ ✳ ✴

☐ Indoor   ☐ Outdoor

Notes

Your Plant's Name: _____

Scientific Name: _____

Date Acquired: _____   *Plant #:* _____

☐ Used Fertilizer?

☐ Pet Friendly?

☐ Indoor   ☐ Outdoor

Water 💧 💧💧 💧💧

Sunlight ☀ ☀ ☀

Notes

Your Plant's Name: _____

Scientific Name: _____

Date Acquired: _____ *Plant #:* _____

☐ **Used Fertilizer?**

☐ **Pet Friendly?**

☐ Indoor ☐ Outdoor

Water 💧 💧💧 💧💧

Sunlight ☀ ☀ ☀

Notes

Your Plant's Name: _____

Scientific Name: _____

Date Acquired: _____ *Plant #:* _____

☐ Used Fertilizer? Water 💧 💧💧 💧💧

☐ Pet Friendly? Sunlight ☀ ☀ ☀

☐ Indoor ☐ Outdoor

Notes

Your Plant's Name: _____

Scientific Name: _____

Date Acquired: _____   *Plant #:* _____

☐ Used Fertilizer?   Water   💧 💧💧 💧💧💧

☐ Pet Friendly?   Sunlight ✶ ✶ ✸

☐ Indoor   ☐ Outdoor

Notes

_____
_____
_____
_____
_____
_____
_____
_____

Your Plant's Name: _____

Scientific Name: _____

Date Acquired: _____   *Plant #:* _____

☐ Used Fertilizer?

☐ Pet Friendly?

☐ Indoor   ☐ Outdoor

Water 💧 💧💧 💧💧

Sunlight ☀ ☀ ☀

Notes

Your Plant's Name: _____

Scientific Name: _____

Date Acquired: _____   *Plant #:* _____

☐ **Used Fertilizer?**

☐ **Pet Friendly?**

☐ Indoor   ☐ Outdoor

Water 💧 💧💧 💧💧💧

Sunlight ☀ ☀ ☀

Notes

Your Plant's Name: _____

Scientific Name: _____

Date Acquired: _____ *Plant #:* _____

☐ Used Fertilizer?

☐ Pet Friendly?

☐ Indoor ☐ Outdoor

Water 💧 💧💧 💧💧

Sunlight ☀ ☀ ☀

Notes

Your Plant's Name: _____

Scientific Name: _____

Date Acquired: _____ *Plant #:* _____

☐ Used Fertilizer? Water 💧 💧💧 💧💧

☐ Pet Friendly? Sunlight ☀ ☀ ☀

☐ Indoor ☐ Outdoor

Notes

Your Plant's Name: _____

Scientific Name: _____

Date Acquired: _____ *Plant #:* _____

☐ Used Fertilizer?

☐ Pet Friendly?

☐ Indoor ☐ Outdoor

Water 💧 💧💧 💧💧

Sunlight ☀ ☀ ☀

Notes

Your Plant's Name: _____

Scientific Name: _____

Date Acquired: _____ *Plant #:* _____

☐ **Used Fertilizer?**   Water   💧 💧💧 💧💧💧

☐ **Pet Friendly?**   Sunlight ☀ ☀ ☀

☐ **Indoor**   ☐ **Outdoor**

Notes

_____
_____
_____
_____
_____
_____
_____
_____

Your Plant's Name: _____

Scientific Name: _____

Date Acquired: _____ *Plant #:* _____

☐ Used Fertilizer?   Water   💧 💧💧 💧💧

☐ Pet Friendly?   Sunlight ☀ ☀ ☀

☐ Indoor   ☐ Outdoor

Notes

Your Plant's Name: _____

Scientific Name: _____

Date Acquired: _____ *Plant #:* _____

☐ Used Fertilizer?

☐ Pet Friendly?

☐ Indoor   ☐ Outdoor

Water   💧 💧💧 💧💧

Sunlight   ☀ ☀ ☀

Notes

Your Plant's Name: _____

Scientific Name: _____

Date Acquired: _____   *Plant #:* _____

☐ Used Fertilizer?

☐ Pet Friendly?

☐ Indoor   ☐ Outdoor

Water 💧 💧💧 💧💧

Sunlight ☀ ☀ ☀

Notes
_____
_____
_____
_____
_____
_____
_____
_____

Your Plant's Name: _____

Scientific Name: _____

Date Acquired: _____   *Plant #:* _____

☐ Used Fertilizer?

☐ Pet Friendly?

☐ Indoor   ☐ Outdoor

Water 💧 💧💧 💧💧

Sunlight ✴ ✴ ✴

Notes

_____
_____
_____
_____
_____
_____
_____
_____

Your Plant's Name: _____

Scientific Name: _____

Date Acquired: _____ *Plant #:* _____

☐ Used Fertilizer?

☐ Pet Friendly?

☐ Indoor ☐ Outdoor

Water 💧 💧💧 💧💧

Sunlight ☀ ☀ ☀

Notes

_____
_____
_____
_____
_____
_____
_____

Your Plant's Name: _____

Scientific Name: _____

Date Acquired: _____   *Plant #:* _____

☐ Used Fertilizer?

☐ Pet Friendly?

☐ Indoor   ☐ Outdoor

Water 💧 💧💧 💧💧

Sunlight ✳ ✳ ✳

Notes

Your Plant's Name: _____

Scientific Name: _____

Date Acquired: _____   *Plant #:* _____

☐ Used Fertilizer?

☐ Pet Friendly?

☐ Indoor   ☐ Outdoor

Water 💧 💧💧 💧💧

Sunlight ☀ ☀ ☀

Notes

_____
_____
_____
_____
_____
_____
_____
_____

Your Plant's Name: _____

Scientific Name: _____

Date Acquired: _____ Plant #: _____

☐ Used Fertilizer?

☐ Pet Friendly?

☐ Indoor ☐ Outdoor

Water 💧 💧💧 💧💧💧

Sunlight ✴ ✴ ✴

Notes

_____
_____
_____
_____
_____
_____
_____
_____

Your Plant's Name: _____

Scientific Name: _____

Date Acquired: _____ *Plant #:* _____

☐ Used Fertilizer?

☐ Pet Friendly?

☐ Indoor ☐ Outdoor

Water 💧 💧💧 💧💧

Sunlight ☀ ☀ ☀

Notes

Your Plant's Name: _____

Scientific Name: _____

Date Acquired: _____ *Plant #:* _____

☐ Used Fertilizer?

☐ Pet Friendly?

☐ Indoor ☐ Outdoor

Water 💧 💧💧 💧💧

Sunlight ☀ ☀ ☀

Notes

_____
_____
_____
_____
_____
_____
_____
_____

Your Plant's Name: _____

Scientific Name: _____

Date Acquired: _____   *Plant #:* _____

☐ Used Fertilizer?

☐ Pet Friendly?

☐ Indoor   ☐ Outdoor

Water 💧 💧💧 💧💧

Sunlight ☀ ☀ ☀

Notes

*There's **always** room for **more** plants...*

- [ ] _____
- [ ] _____
- [ ] _____
- [ ] _____
- [ ] _____
- [ ] _____
- [ ] _____
- [ ] _____
- [ ] _____
- [ ] _____
- [ ] _____
- [ ] _____
- [ ] _____
- [ ] _____

There's **always** room for **more** plants...

- [ ] _____
- [ ] _____
- [ ] _____
- [ ] _____
- [ ] _____
- [ ] _____
- [ ] _____
- [ ] _____
- [ ] _____
- [ ] _____
- [ ] _____
- [ ] _____
- [ ] _____
- [ ] _____

There's **always** room for **more** plants...

- [ ] _____
- [ ] _____
- [ ] _____
- [ ] _____
- [ ] _____
- [ ] _____
- [ ] _____
- [ ] _____
- [ ] _____
- [ ] _____
- [ ] _____
- [ ] _____
- [ ] _____
- [ ] _____

Made in the USA
Monee, IL
09 June 2020